THE GRA(

BIOGRAPHY:

Triumphs and Trials

INKLINE PUBLISHING

Inkline Publishing

Table of Contents

INTRODUCTION

Grace Elizabeth Gold, widely known as Gracie Gold, is a prominent American figure skater whose name is synonymous with excellence on the ice. Born on August 17, 1995, in Newton, Massachusetts, Gracie's journey in the world of figure skating has been adorned with numerous accolades and achievements, solidifying her status as one of the sport's most distinguished athletes.

Throughout her illustrious career, Gracie has etched her name in figure skating history with remarkable accomplishments. She soared to international prominence as a member of the 2014 Olympic team event, clinching the bronze medal in Sochi, Russia. Her stellar performances also secured her victories at prestigious competitions, including the 2014 NHK Trophy and the 2015 Trophée Éric Bompard. In addition to her triumphs on the international stage, Gracie has claimed the title of U.S. national champion twice, in 2014 and 2016, showcasing her dominance within her home country.

Gracie's success extends beyond individual achievements, as she has contributed to Team USA's triumphs at the World Team Trophy, clinching gold in 2013 and 2015. Her impact on the sport transcends borders, as she continues to inspire audiences worldwide with her artistry, athleticism, and unwavering dedication to excellence.

Raised in Springfield, Illinois, Gracie discovered her passion for figure skating at a young age, taking her first steps on the ice in 2003. Under the guidance of coaches Alex Zahradnicek and Pavel Filchenkov, she honed her skills and blossomed into a formidable competitor. Her journey to the elite level of figure skating was punctuated by notable achievements on the junior circuit, including a silver medal at the 2012 World Junior Championships and victories at the 2011 JGP Estonia and the 2012 U.S. junior national championships.

Gracie's groundbreaking achievements include being the first American woman to capture an NHK Trophy title—a testament to her prowess

5

and determination. Moreover, she holds the distinction of achieving the highest short program score ever recorded by an American woman, with an impressive 76.43 points earned at the 2016 World Championships.

Beyond her achievements on the ice, Gracie's journey has been characterized by resilience in the face of adversity. She has courageously confronted mental health challenges, including anxiety and depression, shedding light on the importance of mental well-being in the world of elite athletics. Her openness and vulnerability have sparked important conversations and inspired others to prioritize self-care and seek support when needed.

As Gracie continues to leave an indelible mark on the world of figure skating, her legacy serves as a beacon of hope and inspiration for aspiring athletes and fans alike. With her unparalleled talent, unwavering determination, and unwavering spirit, Gracie Gold embodies the essence of a true champion—both on and off the ice.

Inkline Publishing

EARLY LIFE AND BACKGROUND

Grace Elizabeth Gold, the celebrated figure skater, came into the world on August 17, 1995, in the picturesque town of Newton, Massachusetts. Born to a family deeply rooted in healthcare, Grace is the daughter of Denise, an emergency room nurse, and Carl Gold, an anesthesiologist, both of whom played pivotal roles in shaping her upbringing and fostering her dreams.

Gracie is not alone in her journey; she shares a special bond with her fraternal twin sister, Carly Gold, who entered the world just 40 minutes after Gracie. Carly, named after their father, also found her passion on the ice and ventured into the world of figure skating, showcasing the family's shared love for the sport.

The Gold family's journey took them from the bustling city of Springfield, Missouri, to the vibrant community of Springfield, Illinois, where

Gracie spent her formative years. Along the way, they also made a home in Corpus Christi, Texas, adding a diverse tapestry of experiences to Gracie's upbringing and exposing her to different cultures and environments.

Gracie's pursuit of excellence extended beyond the ice rink; she balanced her passion for figure skating with a commitment to education. In her freshman year, she attended Glenwood High School in Chatham, Illinois, immersing herself in the local community while striving for academic success. Recognizing the demands of her athletic pursuits, Gracie transitioned to online education through the University of Missouri, a testament to her determination to excel both on and off the ice.

In her quest for mastery, Gracie embraced the art of ballet, recognizing its transformative power in enhancing her performance on the ice. With grace and precision, she honed her skills through ballet lessons, harnessing its elegance to elevate her figure skating to new heights.

Gracie's early life was a tapestry woven with dedication, resilience, and unwavering support from her family. From the bustling corridors of hospitals to the serene expanse of ice rinks, her journey reflects a steadfast commitment to excellence and a passion for pursuing her dreams.

Inkline Publishing

11

PERSONAL LIFE

Gracie Elizabeth Gold, born on August 17, 1995, in Newton, Massachusetts, has left an indelible mark on the world of figure skating not just through her accomplishments on the ice, but also through a deeply personal narrative that reflects the human spirit's resilience in the face of profound challenges and setbacks.

Gracie's familial roots are grounded in the medical profession, with her mother Denise serving as an ER nurse and her father Carl as an anesthesiologist. The Gold family expanded with the arrival of fraternal twin sister Carly, born just 40 minutes after Gracie. Both sisters, inspired by their father's name, ventured into the world of figure skating, marking the beginning of a shared passion that would shape their lives.

Raised initially in Springfield, Missouri, Gracie later moved to Springfield, Illinois, and also spent time living in Corpus Christi, Texas. Her academic journey led her to Glenwood High School in Chatham, Illinois, where she attended ninth grade before transitioning to online education through the University of Missouri. Alongside her dedication to figure skating, Gracie explored the world of ballet, recognizing its potential to enhance her on-ice performances.

However, beyond the glittering facade of success lay a personal struggle that Gracie courageously brought into the open. Her battles with anxiety, depression, and an eating disorder became part of her narrative. In 2016, teammate Ashley Wagner urged U.S. Figure Skating officials to intervene, recognizing the signs of Gracie's internal struggles. Despite initial resistance, Gracie eventually sought treatment after a poignant moment in front of judges in 2017.

Moving alone to Michigan in 2017, Gracie faced profound challenges that triggered suicidal thoughts. Isolating herself in her apartment, she found solace and strength in returning to her roots, rediscovering the essence of her love for figure skating. Gracie's openness about her mental health struggles not only contributed to her own healing

13

but also inspired a broader conversation within the figure skating community and beyond.

In her memoir, "Outofshapeworthlessloser: A Memoir of Figure Skating, F*cking Up, and Figuring It Out," released in February 2024, Gracie unveiled another layer of her personal journey. She bravely disclosed an incident of sexual assault by a fellow figure skater at an event after-party when she was twenty-one. Reporting the incident to a U.S. Figure Skating official, she faced a disheartening delay in receiving acknowledgment from the organization, highlighting systemic issues in addressing such cases within the sport.

Despite these deeply personal challenges, Gracie continued to redefine her goals and sought a healthier approach to figure skating. In December 2019, she reflected on her journey, acknowledging the progress she had made and expressing a resilient spirit: "Yes, things could be better, but look how far I've come."

Amidst the tumultuous tides of her personal journey, Gracie found refuge and strength in the embrace of love. Her relationship with James Hernandez, blossoming amidst the backdrop of their shared passion for ice sports, became a cornerstone of support and companionship. Together, they navigated the challenges and triumphs of life, finding solace in each other's presence and unwavering support.

As Gracie's journey unfolded, her resilience and courage continued to inspire others. In 2020, she became a prominent figure in the HBO Sports Documentary, "The Weight of Gold," which shed light on the mental health challenges faced by Olympic athletes. By sharing her own struggles with anxiety, depression, and disordered eating, Gracie contributed to a broader dialogue about the importance of prioritizing mental well-being in the pursuit of athletic excellence.

Beyond the confines of her athletic career, Gracie's advocacy for mental health awareness extended to her memoir, a candid account of her journey titled "Outofshapeworthlessloser: A

Memoir of Figure Skating, F*cking Up, and Figuring It Out." In this raw and unfiltered narrative, she courageously shared her experiences, including instances of sexual assault and the subsequent challenges in seeking justice within the figure skating community.

Gracie's willingness to confront and navigate the complexities of her personal journey resonated deeply with audiences, sparking conversations and fostering a greater sense of empathy and understanding. Her unwavering commitment to authenticity and vulnerability became a beacon of hope for those grappling with their own inner demons, reminding them that they are not alone in their struggles.

In the midst of her personal challenges, Gracie's resilience on the ice remained a testament to her unwavering dedication and passion for figure skating. Despite setbacks and obstacles, she continued to pursue her dreams with unwavering determination, finding solace and strength in the sport that had been her lifelong passion.

As she continues to navigate the complexities of her personal and professional journey, Gracie remains a symbol of resilience, courage, and unwavering determination. Her willingness to confront adversity with grace and authenticity serves as an inspiration to all who encounter her story, reminding us of the transformative power of perseverance and the indomitable spirit of the human heart.

In the realm of love and companionship, Gracie found solace and strength in her relationship with James Hernandez. Their shared passion for ice sports provided a foundation of mutual understanding and support, fostering a connection that served as a source of comfort and resilience amidst life's challenges.

Through her advocacy for mental health awareness and her willingness to share her own struggles, Gracie became a beacon of hope for countless individuals grappling with similar issues. Her courage in confronting adversity with grace and vulnerability inspired a broader conversation about the importance of prioritizing mental well-being in the pursuit of athletic excellence.

As Gracie's journey continues to unfold, her resilience and unwavering commitment to authenticity serve as a reminder of the power of the human spirit to triumph over adversity. In her story, we find echoes of our own struggles and triumphs, a testament to the resilience that resides within each of us, waiting to be unleashed in the pursuit of our dreams.

Beyond the confines of the ice rink, Gracie Gold's personal life serves as a testament to the complexities and triumphs inherent in the human experience. Her courage in facing and sharing her struggles has not only shaped her own narrative but has also contributed to a broader conversation about mental health and well-being within the demanding world of elite sports. In the face of adversity, Gracie's journey remains a source of inspiration and a reminder of the resilience that resides within us all.

Inkline Publishing

19

FIGURE SKATING CAREER BEGINNINGS

Gracie Gold's initiation into the enchanting world of figure skating unfolded in a serendipitous manner when, at the age of 8, she attended a friend's birthday party at a local rink in Springfield, Missouri. Little did she anticipate that this casual outing would not only introduce her to the glacial expanse of the ice but also serve as the catalyst for a journey that would redefine the contours of her life.

Under the initial guidance of coaches Amy Vorhaben and Max Liu, Gracie's early days in figure skating were marked by a sense of wonder and the joy of discovery. These foundational experiences paved the way for her later successes as she learned the intricacies of the sport, developing a connection with the ice that would become integral to her identity.

As Gracie's aspirations soared, so did the roster of coaches who contributed to shaping her trajectory.

The transition to working with Alexia Griffin marked a crucial juncture in her development, where Gracie not only refined her technical prowess but also began to embrace the artistic nuances that define figure skating as a form of expression.

Her journey, however, was not confined to a single locale. The pursuit of excellence took Gracie from Missouri to Springfield, Illinois, where Susan Liss became her new guiding force. Under Liss's mentorship, Gracie continued to evolve as a skater, absorbing the wisdom and techniques that would set the stage for her future endeavors.

A pivotal chapter in Gracie's early career unfolded under the tutelage of Toni Hickey. The move to Hickey's guidance in Springfield, Illinois, marked a period of intensive training and strategic refinement of her skills. With each coaching transition, Gracie absorbed invaluable lessons, drawing inspiration from the diverse perspectives that enriched her approach to figure skating.

The narrative of Gracie's skating journey extended beyond state lines, reaching the bustling skating community of the Chicago area. Here, she found a mentor in Alex Ouriashev, whose influence spanned across two rinks. Under Ouriashev's watchful eye, Gracie's abilities reached new heights as she delved into the intricacies of her craft, absorbing the nuances that would distinguish her on the competitive stage.

A testament to her versatility, Gracie ventured into pairs skating with Sean Hickey, a partnership that showcased her ability to navigate different facets of the sport. Their joint efforts culminated in an impressive eighth-place finish in juvenile pairs at the 2007 U.S. Junior Championships, laying the groundwork for Gracie's future successes as a solo skater.

However, the journey was not without its trials. A fourth-place finish on the novice level at the 2010 U.S. Championships hinted at the challenges that accompany competitive skating. Undeterred, Gracie elevated her ambitions, transitioning to the junior level the following season. Yet, a setback at the Midwestern Sectionals saw her finish sixth, falling short of the national championships.

Rather than succumb to disappointment, Gracie embraced these moments as opportunities for growth. Recognizing the need for increased technical prowess, she devoted herself to intensive preparation, laying the groundwork for the following season with a commitment to elevating her skill set.

In the tapestry of Gracie's early figure skating career, each coaching transition, every competition, and setback played a crucial role in shaping the athlete she was becoming. Her resilience in the face of challenges and her unwavering commitment to improvement set the stage for the chapters that lay ahead, as Gracie Gold prepared to leave an indelible mark on the world of figure skating.

COMPETITIVE SUCCESSES

International Debut 2011-2012:

In the 2011–12 season, Gold made her international debut at the Junior Grand Prix in Tallinn, Estonia, securing the top spot. She subsequently earned a place in the 2012 U.S. Championships on the junior level, where she clinched both the short and long programs to claim the gold medal. Notably, her total score of 178.92 points set a new record for a junior lady at the U.S. Championships. Throughout the season leading up to the U.S. Championships, Gold dominated by winning gold in all seven of her competitions. She then represented the United States at the 2012 World Junior Championships in Minsk, Belarus, where she achieved the silver medal. Following her success, she signed with International Management Group. Additionally, Gold was selected for the U.S. team for the 2012 World Team Trophy, where she made her senior international debut, finishing fifth overall, with

24

Team USA securing second place overall, led by fellow Junior Worlds medalist Adelina Sotnikova.

Senior Debut 2012-13:

Gold debuted in the senior Grand Prix circuit during the 2012 Skate Canada, where she finished seventh. Following this, she collaborated with a sports psychologist to enhance her focus and fine-tune her routines in Canton, Michigan. Subsequently, at her next competition, the 2012 Rostelecom Cup, she secured the silver medal. Making her debut at the senior U.S. Nationals, Gold placed ninth in the short program but rallied to clinch first in the free skate, earning her the silver medal overall with a total score of 186.57 points. This performance earned her a spot at the 2013 Four Continents, where she finished sixth. At the 2013 World Championships, she impressed with a ninth-place finish in the short program, fifth in the free skate, and sixth overall, achieving a new personal best total score of 184.25 points. Notably, her sixth-place finish, combined with teammate Ashley Wagner's fifth-place finish, secured three spots for U.S. women at the 2014 Winter Olympics. During the 2013 World Team Trophy in Tokyo, Gold excelled by placing third in both the short program and free skate, securing third place overall with a personal and season-best total score of 188.03 points. Team USA also emerged victorious, earning the team gold for the second time since 2009. Additionally, in July 2013, Gold was appointed as a Pandora Jewelry ambassador.

First national title & Olympic medal 2013-14:

Following her split with coach Alex Ourashiev in late August 2013, Gold began training under Marina Zoueva and Oleg Epstein in Canton, Michigan, while also seeking a permanent coach. She secured the silver medal at her initial event of the season, the U.S. International Figure Skating Classic. Following the competition, she headed to California for a week-long assessment with Frank Carroll at the Toyota Sports Center in El Segundo. On September 25, 2013, it was confirmed that Carroll would become her permanent coach.

Throughout the 2013–14 ISU Grand Prix series, Gold participated in the 2013 Skate Canada, where she attained first place in the short program with a personal best score of 69.45 and third place in the free skate, ultimately earning the bronze medal overall. In the 2013 NHK Trophy, she finished fourth and was designated as the third alternate for the Grand Prix Final.

At the 2014 U.S. Championships, Gold excelled by achieving first place in the short program with 72.12 points, marking the highest-ever ladies' score recorded at the U.S. Championships under the ISU Judging System. Subsequently, she triumphed in the free skate with another record-breaking score of 139.57, thus securing her inaugural senior national title. Consequently, she was selected for the U.S. team for the 2014 Winter Olympics in Sochi, Russia. In the Olympic team event, she earned a bronze medal, but controversially placed fourth and missed the podium in the ladies' singles event with a score of 205.53 points. Despite this, Gold was assigned to compete at the 2014 World Championships in Saitama, Japan, where she finished fifth overall. To conclude the season, she performed with Stars On Ice.

NHK Trophy Title (2014–15 season):

Gold commenced her season at the 2014 Nebelhorn Trophy, an ISU Challenger Series event, where she secured the bronze medal behind

Russians Elizaveta Tuktamysheva and Alena Leonova. In the 2014–15 ISU Grand Prix season, Gold was assigned to compete at the 2014 Skate America and the 2014 NHK Trophy.

She attained bronze at Skate America and captured gold at the NHK Trophy, marking her maiden victory at a Grand Prix event and the first time an American woman had won the NHK Trophy. Consequently, she qualified for her inaugural Grand Prix Final, but withdrew on December 4, 2014, due to a stress fracture in her left foot.

At the 2015 U.S. Championships, Gold clinched a silver medal with a score of 205.54 after securing second place in both the short program and free skate. In the 2015 Four Continents Championships, she positioned second in the short program with a score of 62.67 but dropped to fifth in the free skate with a score of 113.91, ultimately finishing fourth overall with a total score of 176.58.

During the 2015 World Championships, Gold achieved eighth place in the short program with a score of 60.73, her lowest score of the season. However, she rebounded in the free skate with a score of 128.23, her season's best and the second highest free skate score of the ladies' event, securing fourth place overall, her best placement at a World Championship thus far.

Gold represented Team USA at the 2015 World Team Trophy, clinching first place in the short program with a score of 71.26, the highest score ever recorded for an American woman in an ISU event. Nonetheless, she landed in fifth place in the free skate, but overall Team USA secured first place.

In the 2015–16 season, Gold's Grand Prix Series assignments were the 2015 Skate America and 2015 Trophée Éric Bompard. She earned the silver medal at Skate America, trailing behind Russia's Evgenia Medvedeva. Later, at Trophée Éric Bompard, she secured first place in the short program with a score of 73.32.

Unfortunately, the event was canceled on November 14 due to the state of emergency in France following the November 2015 Paris attacks. The ISU announced on November 23 that the short program standings would stand as final placements, securing Gold a spot in the 2015 Grand Prix Final, where she placed fifth in both the short and free programs, ultimately ranking fifth overall.

On January 23, Gold claimed her second National title at the 2016 U.S. Championships in Saint Paul, Minnesota. Following her national victory, she landed in fifth place at the 2016 Four Continents Championships in Taipei, Taiwan.

Subsequently, Gold participated in the 2016 World Championships in Boston, securing first place in the short program with a score of 76.43, the highest short program score ever recorded by an American woman. Despite placing sixth in the free program, she dropped to fourth place overall. To conclude her season, Gold competed at the inaugural 2016 KOSÉ Team Challenge Cup, contributing to Team North America's gold medal victory.

Second National Title (2015–16 season):

In the 2015–16 Grand Prix Series, Gold was assigned to compete at the 2015 Skate America and 2015 Trophée Éric Bompard. At Skate America, she earned the silver medal, trailing behind Russia's Evgenia Medvedeva. Continuing her season, Gold secured first place in the short program at Trophée Éric Bompard with a score of 73.32.

However, the event was called off on November 14 due to the state of emergency in France following the November 2015 Paris attacks. Subsequently, on November 23, the ISU declared that the short program standings would serve as final placements. This ensured Gold's participation in the 2015 Grand Prix Final, where she finished 5th in both the short and free programs, ultimately ranking 5th overall.

On January 23, Gold claimed her second National title at the 2016 U.S. Championships in Saint Paul, Minnesota. Following her national victory, she placed fifth at the 2016 Four Continents Championships in Taipei, Taiwan.

Gold then competed at the 2016 World Championships in Boston, where she secured first place in the short program with a score of 76.43, the highest ever recorded by an American woman. Despite placing sixth in the free program, she finished fourth overall. To conclude her season, Gold participated in the inaugural 2016 KOSÉ Team Challenge Cup, contributing to Team North America's gold medal victory.

CHALLENGES AND SETBACKS

Gracie Gold's journey in figure skating is a testament to her extraordinary talent and resilience, yet it has also been fraught with formidable challenges and setbacks that have tested her resolve like never before. Despite her exceptional skill and unwavering dedication, Gracie found herself grappling with a series of obstacles that threatened to derail her career and shake her to her core.

As Gracie embarked on the 2016 season, she was assigned to two prestigious Grand Prix events, Skate America and Trophée de France, marking the beginning of what should have been a promising season. However, her aspirations were soon overshadowed by a string of disappointments and setbacks that would come to define this tumultuous chapter in her career.

The season began with the 2016 Japan Open, where Gracie's performance in the free skate fell short of her usual standards, earning her a score of 108.24. While she contributed to Team North America's bronze medal win, it was clear that all was not well. The cracks began to show at 2016 Skate America, where Gracie's third-place finish in the short program was marred by a fall on her triple flip. Despite her best efforts, she struggled in the free skate, suffering multiple falls and ultimately dropping to fifth place overall with a total score of 184.22. Gracie attributed her subpar performance to "post-worlds summer depression," revealing that she had only recently begun to feel like herself again.

Unfortunately, Gracie's struggles continued at the 2016 Trophée de France, where she endured yet another disappointing finish, scoring a combined total of 165.89 for eighth place, the worst Grand Prix finish of her career. As the season drew to a close, it became increasingly clear that Gracie was facing challenges that extended beyond the realm of competition.

In late December 2016, Gracie made the difficult decision to resume her collaboration with her former coach, Alex Ouriashev, seeking refuge in familiar surroundings as she grappled with the uncertainties of her career. However, her efforts to regain her footing were met with further setbacks as she finished sixth at the 2017 U.S. Championships, a far cry from her previous successes. To make matters worse, Gracie was left off the Four Continents and World Championship teams for the first time in her senior career, marking a devastating blow to her aspirations.

The turmoil continued as Gracie found herself embroiled in a public controversy surrounding her coaching arrangements. Following the U.S. Championships, her coach Frank Carroll announced their decision to part ways to the media before informing Gracie, causing uproar on social media. Despite the upheaval, Gracie remained steadfast in her resolve to navigate the challenges ahead, expressing her utmost respect for Carroll and taking the time to evaluate her coaching options as she prepared for the Olympic season.

In February 2017, Gracie announced that Marina Zoueva and Oleg Epstein would be her trainers at the Arctic Edge ice rink in Canton, Michigan, marking yet another chapter in her quest for stability and success in the sport. However, her journey was further complicated by allegations of pressure from sponsors, including Nike, to maintain an excessively thin physique, exacerbating her struggles with disordered eating and mental health issues.

The 2017-2018 season proved to be a continuation of Gracie's battle with personal demons and mental health challenges. She withdrew from the Japan Open and the CS Ondrej Nepela Trophy due to personal reasons, signaling the depths of her struggles. Despite being assigned to two Grand Prix events, Gracie withdrew from both the 2017 Cup of China and the 2017 Internationaux de France in October, citing ongoing treatment for anxiety, depression, and an eating disorder. Her decision to withdraw from the U.S. Nationals underscored the severity of her situation, as she acknowledged that she would not have proper training beforehand.

As the season drew to a close, Gracie's future in the sport remained uncertain. Reports surfaced that she had been hired as a coach in Arizona, signaling a potential shift in her career trajectory. Despite the challenges and setbacks she faced, Gracie's resilience and determination remained unwavering, a testament to her indomitable spirit and unwavering commitment to overcoming adversity.

Inkline Publishing

39

COMEBACK ATTEMPTS

Gracie Gold's return to competitive figure skating following a period of personal struggles and setbacks stands as a testament to the resilience of the human spirit and the unwavering determination to overcome adversity. With each graceful glide and elegant performance, she embarked on a journey of redemption, seeking to reclaim her rightful place on the ice and redefine her legacy in the sport she loves.

The 2018–19 season marked the beginning of Gracie's comeback journey, as she announced her return to competitive skating with an assignment to the prestigious Rostelecom Cup. Under the guidance of coach Vincent Restencourt and with choreography by former skater Jeremy Abbott, Gracie unveiled new programs that reflected her personal journey of triumph and resilience. Despite facing challenges in the short program at the Rostelecom Cup, Gracie's decision to withdraw from the free skate demonstrated a newfound commitment to prioritizing her mental health and well-being above all else.

As she continued to prepare for the upcoming season and set her sights on the 2022 Winter Olympics in Beijing, Gracie embarked on a rigorous training regimen aimed at refining her skills and mastering new elements. Videos shared by her coach on social media showcased Gracie's determination and progress, as she began to execute jumps with precision and confidence, laying the foundation for her future success on the ice.

The 2019–2020 season saw Gracie's return to domestic regional competitions as she sought to earn a coveted spot at the U.S. Championships. Despite facing formidable competition and significant errors in her performances, Gracie's resilience and determination shone through as she secured a bronze medal at the Eastern Sectional Championships, thus earning her a qualifying spot for the national championships.

In the following season, Gracie's inclusion in U.S. Figure Skating's international selection pool offered her the opportunity to compete at prestigious events, including the 2020 Skate America. Despite facing challenges on the ice, Gracie's unwavering commitment to her craft and her willingness to push the boundaries of her abilities served as a testament to her resilience and determination.

As the 2021–2022 season unfolded, Gracie continued to showcase her competitive spirit and unwavering dedication to the sport. Despite facing setbacks at the U.S. Championships, her resolve remained unshaken as she set her sights on the future and the opportunities that lay ahead.

Approaching the 2022–2023 season with renewed determination and a hunger for success, Gracie embarked on a quest to redefine her narrative and prove herself as a formidable competitor on the international stage. Her bronze medal win at the Philadelphia Summer International, coupled with impressive performances at the CS Nebelhorn

Trophy and Skate America, underscored her continued growth and evolution as a skater.

At the 2023 U.S. Figure Skating Championships, Gracie once again demonstrated her resilience and determination, delivering standout performances that showcased her skill and artistry on the ice. Despite facing challenges in the free skate, her fifth-place finish in the short program and eighth-place overall marked a significant milestone in her comeback journey, signaling her return to competitive form and setting the stage for future success.

As Gracie's comeback attempts continue to unfold, her journey serves as a powerful reminder of the transformative power of perseverance, resilience, and unwavering determination in the face of adversity. With each graceful glide and elegant performance, she inspires audiences around the world and leaves an indelible mark on the sport she loves, proving that with dedication, passion, and unwavering belief in oneself, anything is possible.

LEGACY AND IMPACT

Gracie Gold's impact on the world of figure skating transcends mere athletic achievements, resonating deeply with audiences worldwide through her remarkable journey of triumph, resilience, and advocacy. Delving into her legacy reveals a profound narrative of courage, vulnerability, and unwavering determination that has left an indelible mark on the sport and inspired countless individuals to confront their own challenges with grace and resilience.

At the heart of Gracie's legacy lies her unwavering commitment to authenticity and openness, particularly regarding her struggles with mental health. By courageously sharing her battles with anxiety, depression, and disordered eating, Gracie sparked a vital conversation within the figure skating community and beyond about the importance of prioritizing mental well-being in the pursuit of athletic excellence. Her willingness to confront taboo subjects and advocate for greater support and understanding

44

for those grappling with similar issues has transformed her into a beacon of hope and inspiration for countless individuals facing their own internal struggles.

Gracie's impact extends far beyond her athletic achievements, reaching audiences around the globe through her advocacy efforts and willingness to confront systemic issues within the figure skating community. In her memoir and public statements, Gracie shed light on the challenges faced by athletes, including instances of sexual assault, and called for greater accountability and support for survivors. Her fearless stance against injustice and her unwavering commitment to speaking truth to power have earned her admiration and respect from fans and fellow athletes alike.

Furthermore, Gracie's resilience and determination in the face of adversity have inspired countless individuals to persevere in the pursuit of their dreams, no matter the obstacles they may encounter. Her comeback attempts, marked by setbacks and challenges, serve as a

45

testament to the power of perseverance and the unwavering belief in oneself to overcome even the most daunting of obstacles. Through her actions and words, Gracie has shown that setbacks are not the end of the road but rather opportunities for growth, resilience, and transformation.

Gracie's legacy is also deeply intertwined with her artistry and athleticism on the ice. With her graceful movements and impeccable technique, she captivated audiences worldwide and earned admiration from fans and fellow athletes alike. Her performances, characterized by passion, precision, and poise, left an indelible impression on all who had the privilege of witnessing her grace the ice, further solidifying her status as an icon within the sport.

As Gracie's journey continues to unfold, her legacy remains a source of inspiration and empowerment for generations to come. Whether she is advocating for mental health awareness, confronting injustice, or dazzling audiences with her performances, Gracie's impact on the world of figure skating and beyond is undeniable. Her

46

resilience, courage, and unwavering determination serve as a reminder that no obstacle is insurmountable and that with dedication, passion, and belief in oneself, anything is possible.

In the annals of figure skating history, Gracie Gold's name will forever be synonymous with resilience, courage, and the enduring power of the human spirit. Her legacy stands as a testament to the transformative power of perseverance, authenticity, and unwavering determination, inspiring future generations of athletes to pursue their dreams with grace, resilience, and unwavering belief in themselves.

ENDORSEMENT

Gracie Gold's influence extends beyond the ice rink, as evidenced by her impressive array of endorsements and ambassadorships. In October 2013, Gold was announced as one of the faces of CoverGirl, a prestigious cosmetic brand. This endorsement marked a significant milestone in her career, elevating her profile to a global audience.

Her captivating presence caught the attention of renowned publications, earning her coveted spots on the covers of Sports Illustrated's February 2014 issue, GQ Japan, and Teen Vogue. These appearances not only showcased her athletic prowess but also underscored her status as a fashion icon and cultural influencer.

Furthermore, Gracie's exceptional achievements in the world of sports earned her recognition beyond the skating community. In 2014, she was honored as the Sportswoman of the Year by the Los Angeles Council, a testament to her widespread impact and influence. This accolade was bestowed upon her during the prestigious

L.A. Sports ceremony in March of the same year, solidifying her status as a revered figure in the sporting world.

Gracie's endorsement portfolio also includes an ambassadorship for KOSÉ Infinity beauty products, highlighting her versatility and appeal beyond the realm of athletics. As an ambassador, she embodies the brand's values of beauty, elegance, and sophistication, further enhancing her reputation as a role model and influencer.

In addition to her beauty and fashion endorsements, Gracie has secured partnerships with leading brands in the skating industry. She is sponsored by John Wilson, the manufacturer of her skating blades, Pattern-99, where she serves as the brand ambassador. Her collaboration with Edea, her skating boot manufacturer, showcases her commitment to excellence and innovation in her craft.

Gracie's endorsement roster extends beyond the world of sports and fashion, encompassing partnerships with global brands such as Visa,

United Airlines, Procter & Gamble, Red Bull, and Nike. These partnerships not only attest to her marketability and appeal but also underscore her ability to transcend boundaries and resonate with diverse audiences worldwide.

Overall, Gracie Gold's endorsements reflect her multifaceted appeal and influence as an athlete, fashion icon, and cultural influencer. Through her partnerships with prestigious brands and ambassadorships, she continues to inspire and empower individuals worldwide, leaving an indelible mark on the worlds of sports, fashion, and beauty.

Inkline Publishing

CONCLUSION

In wrapping up Gracie Gold's profound journey within the realm of figure skating, it becomes evident that her narrative surpasses mere athletic achievement; it embodies the epitome of human resilience amidst adversity. From her modest beginnings to the pinnacle of competitive success, Gracie's saga emerges as a narrative of fortitude, perseverance, and unyielding determination.

Over the course of her illustrious career, Gracie has encountered a plethora of challenges, both on and off the ice. From grappling with mental health tribulations to confronting systemic injustices ingrained within the sport, she has consistently embraced transparency and advocated for change. Her fearlessness in addressing taboo subjects and divulging her vulnerabilities has not only provided solace to countless individuals navigating similar struggles but has also catalyzed crucial dialogues concerning the paramount importance of prioritizing mental well-being in the pursuit of excellence.

Gracie's influence transcends the boundaries of the skating rink, resonating with audiences worldwide through her activism and steadfast commitment to authenticity. Her resilience in the face of adversity serves as an emblem of hope and inspiration for all those who encounter her narrative, underscoring the truth that no obstacle is insurmountable, and with unwavering determination, passion, and self-belief, the realm of possibilities knows no bounds.

As Gracie traverses the peaks and valleys of her journey, her legacy endures as a testament to the transformative potency of perseverance and the enduring vigor of the human spirit. Within her tenacity, courage, and resolute resolve, individuals discover echoes of their own trials and triumphs, serving as a poignant reminder that with resilience, perseverance, and authenticity, one can surmount even the most formidable of challenges.

In the annals of figure skating history, Gracie Gold's appellation is forever etched as a symbol of resilience, courage, and an unwavering pursuit of excellence. Her narrative serves as a poignant reminder that genuine greatness is not solely gauged by victories but rather by the mettle of character forged amidst the crucible of adversity. As we bid adieu to this chapter of her odyssey, we eagerly anticipate the next, cognizant that irrespective of what the future holds, Gracie's legacy will persist in inspiring and uplifting individuals across the globe.